Pebble Plus

LET'S LOOK AT COUNTRIES

LET'S LOOK AT CHINA

BY MARY MEINKING

raintree
a Capstone company — publishers for children

Raintree is an imprint of Capstone Global Library Limited, a company incorporated in England and Wales having its registered office at 264 Banbury Road, Oxford, OX2 7DY – Registered company number: 6695582

www.raintree.co.uk
myorders@raintree.co.uk

Text © Capstone Global Library Limited 2020
The moral rights of the proprietor have been asserted.

All rights reserved. No part of this publication may be reproduced in any form or by any means (including photocopying or storing it in any medium by electronic means and whether or not transiently or incidentally to some other use of this publication) without the written permission of the copyright owner, except in accordance with the provisions of the Copyright, Designs and Patents Act 1988 or under the terms of a licence issued by the Copyright Licensing Agency, Barnard's Inn, 86 Fetter Lane, London, EC4A 1EN (www.cla.co.uk). Applications for the copyright owner's written permission should be addressed to the publisher.

Edited by Jessica Server
Designed by Juliette Peters
Picture research by Jo Miller
Production by Laura Manthe
Originated by Capstone Global Library Ltd
Printed and bound in India

ISBN 978 1 4747 8445 0 (hardback)
ISBN 978 1 4747 8462 7 (paperback)

British Library Cataloguing in Publication Data
A full catalogue record for this book is available from the British Library.

Photo Credits
Newscom: Minden Pictures/Thomas Marent, 9; Shutterstock: Anton Watman, 8, bonchan, 13, chuyuss, 6-7, Globe Turner, 22 (Inset), HelloRF Zcool, Cover Top, Hung Chung Chih, Cover Middle, JekLi, 22-23, 24, Monkey Business Images, 11, nale, 4 (map), natsunee matchika, 18-19, Perfect Gui, 1, plavevski, 17, Roman Kosolapov, 21, SeaSandSun, 2-3, Songquan Deng, 4-5, superjoseph, Cover Bottom, Cover Back, testing, 15, Zhao jian kang, 16

Every effort has been made to contact copyright holders of material reproduced in this book. Any omissions will be rectified in subsequent printings if notice is given to the publisher.

All the internet addresses (URLs) given in this book were valid at the time of going to press. However, due to the dynamic nature of the internet, some addresses may have changed, or sites may have changed or ceased to exist since publication. While the author and publisher regret any inconvenience this may cause readers, no responsibility for any such changes can be accepted by either the author or the publisher.

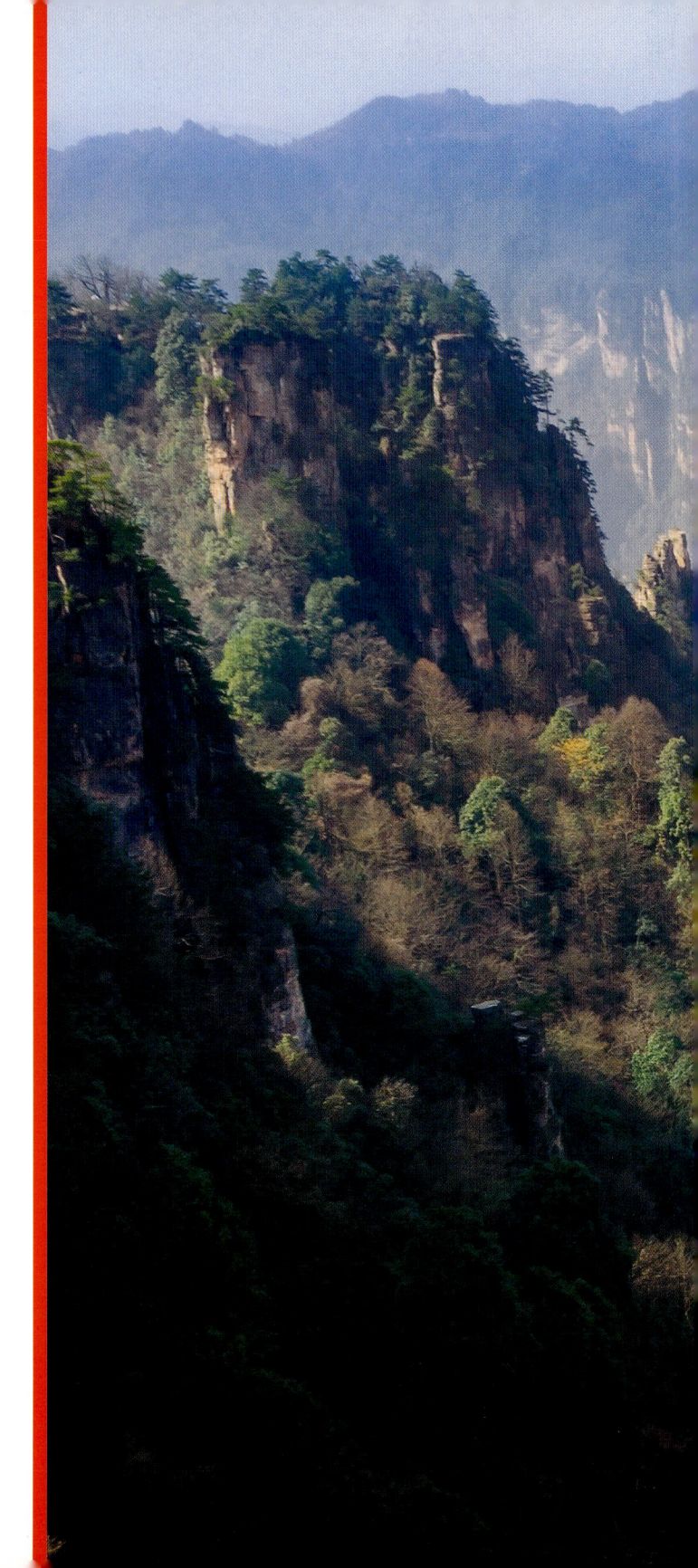

CONTENTS

Where is China? 4
From mountains to deserts 6
In the wild 8
People 10
At the table 12
Festivals 14
At work 16
Transport 18
Famous place 20

Quick China facts 22
Glossary 22
Find out more 23
Comprehension questions 24
Index 24

Where is China?

China is in eastern Asia. It is almost as big as the whole of Europe. China's capital city is Beijing.

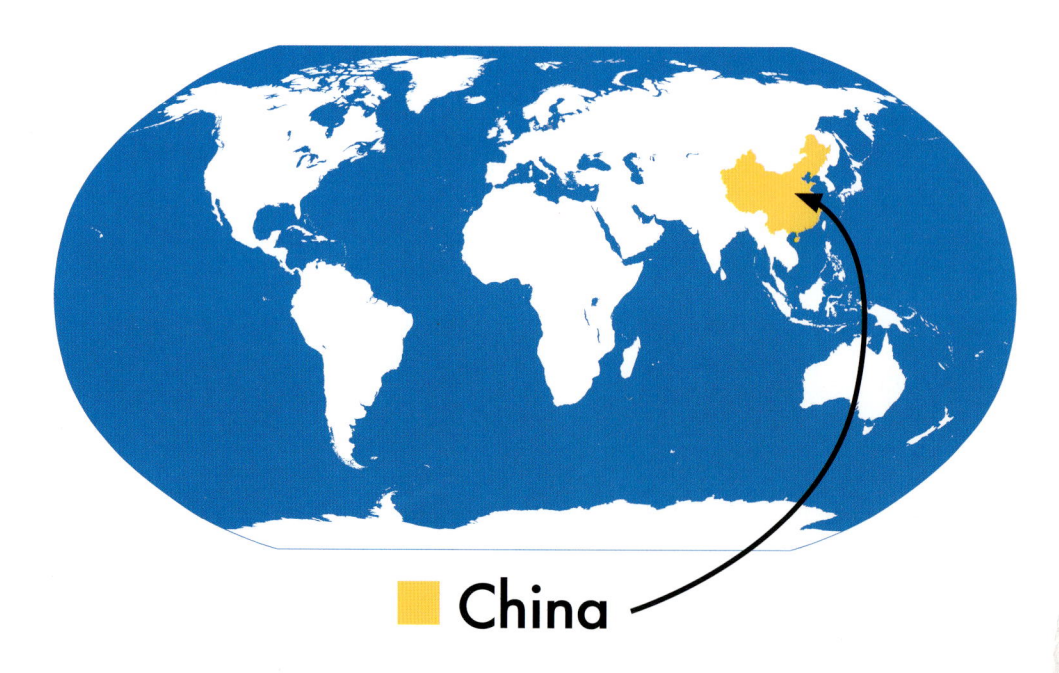

◼ China

Beijing

From mountains to deserts

High mountains cover much of China. There are hot deserts in the north. Long rivers run across the country. They flow into different seas.

Li river

In the wild

Rare animals live in China. Giant pandas live in the bamboo forests. Golden snub-nosed monkeys hide in the trees. Snow leopards roam in the mountains.

giant panda

golden snub-nosed monkeys

People

People have lived in China for a long time. The Han people lived in China thousands of years ago. They were farmers, artists and scientists. Today most Chinese people have Han ancestors.

11

At the table

Rice and noodles are common foods in China. So are stir-fry vegetables and meats. People use chopsticks instead of forks. Meals often begin or end with soup.

chopsticks

Festivals

China's biggest festival is Chinese New Year. People eat special food together, such as dumplings and raw fish salad. At night they set off fireworks. People dance and dress up as dragons and lions.

15

At work

Many Chinese people work on farms. They grow crops and raise animals. Many others make toys, electronics and clothing in factories. The products are sold around the world.

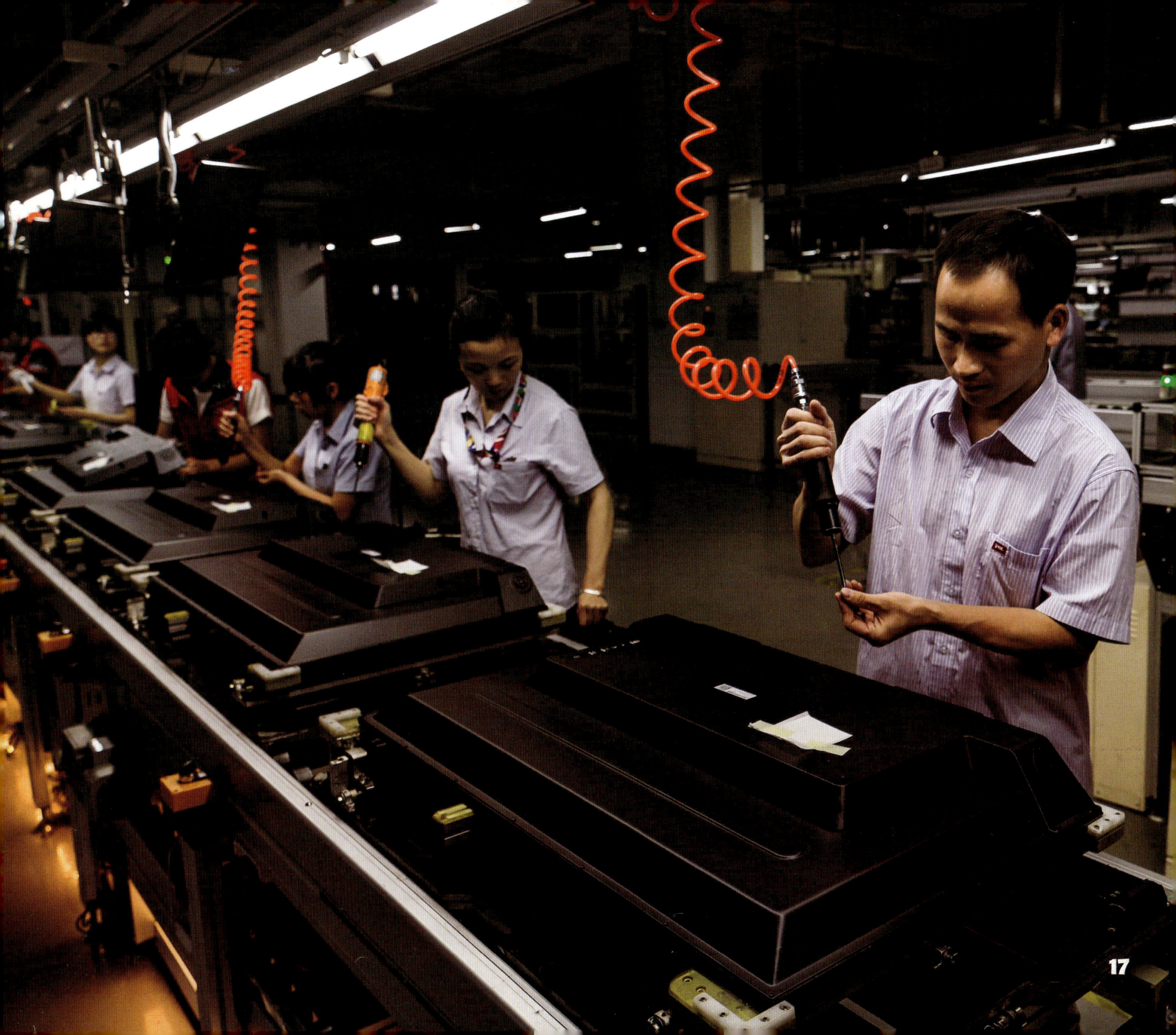

Transport

Many people in China travel by train. Railway tracks cross the country. Some trains use magnets to make them move very fast. Cities also have buses, taxis and underground trains.

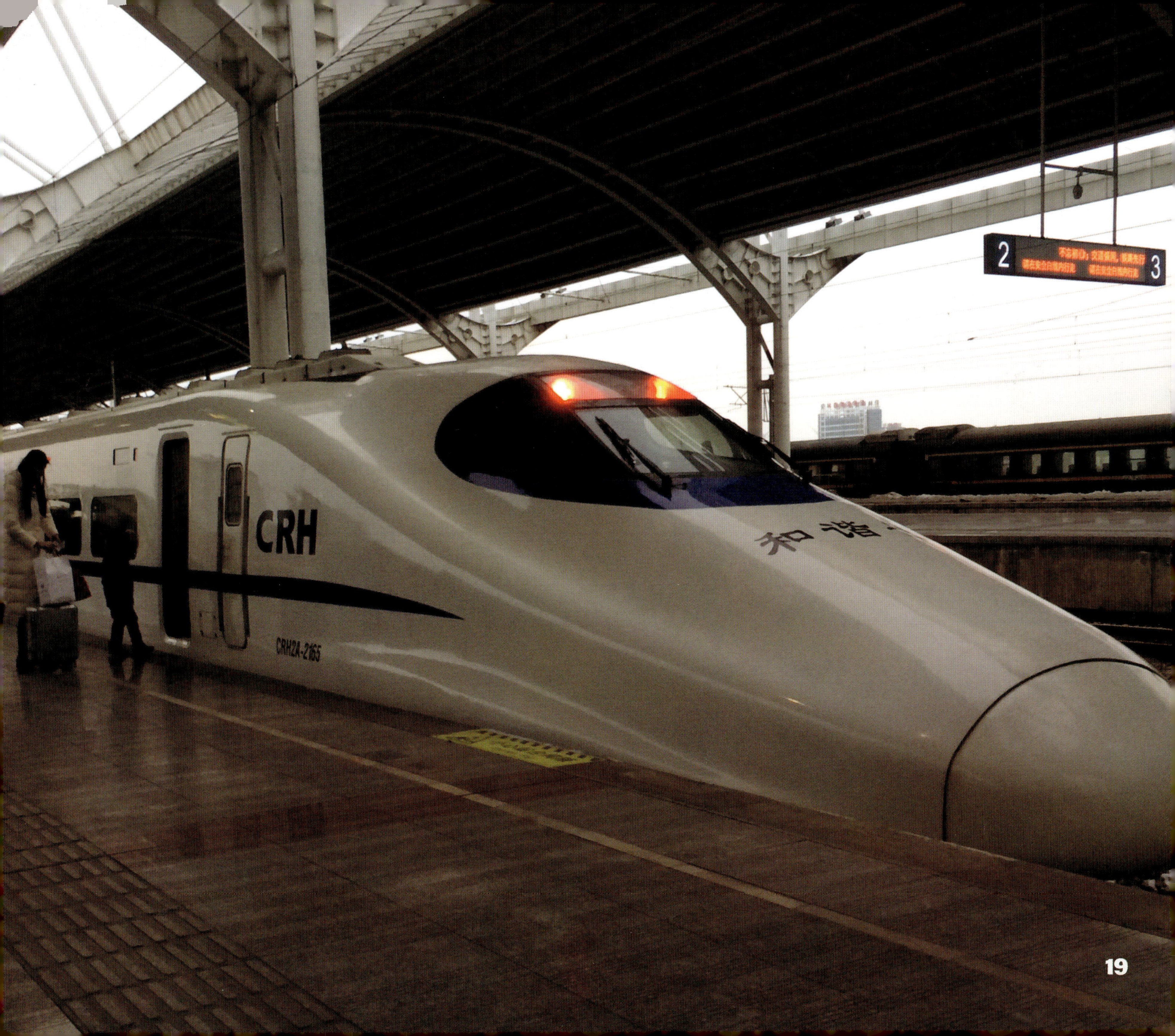
CRH
CRH2A-2165
和谐

Famous place

Many tourists visit the Great Wall of China. Workers built it near China's northern border more than 2,000 years ago. It was built to keep out China's enemies.

21

QUICK CHINA FACTS

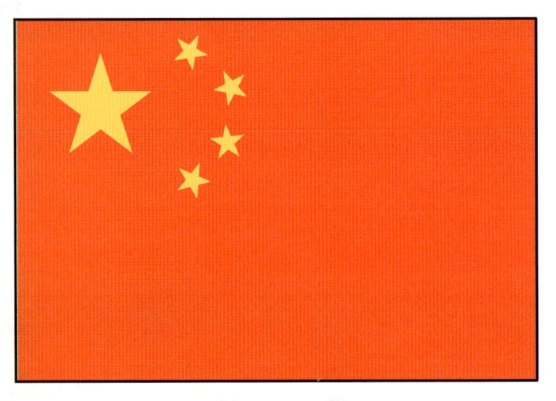

China's flag

Name: The People's Republic of China
Capital: Beijing
Other major cities: Guangzhou, Shanghai, Chongqing
Population: 1,384,688,986 (July 2018 estimate)
Size: 9,596,960 sq km (3,705,406 square miles)
Main languages: Mandarin Chinese, Cantonese
Money: Chinese yuan

GLOSSARY

ancestor a family member who lived a long time ago

bamboo a tropical grass with a hard, hollow stem

border a dividing line between two places

capital the city in a country where the government is based

chopsticks two narrow sticks used to eat food; chopsticks are used mostly by people in Asian countries

crop a plant that farmers grow in large amounts, usually for food; farmers grow crops such as rice, soybeans and wheat

rare not often seen, found or happening

stir-fry cooking food quickly over a high heat

FIND OUT MORE

Books

China (Country Guides with Benjamin Blog and his Inquisitive Dog), Anita Ganeri (Raintree, 2014)

China (Usborne Beginners), Leonie Pratt (Usborne, 2008)

Chinese New Year (Holidays Around the World), Lisa J. Amstutz (Raintree, 2017)

Websites

All you want to know about the Great Wall of China, China's most famous site
www.sciencekids.co.nz/sciencefacts/engineering/greatwallofchina.html

More cool facts about China and lots of other countries too!
www.natgeokids.com/uk/?s=china

COMPREHENSION QUESTIONS

1. What rare animals live in China? Which would you most like to see?

2. What types of jobs do many Chinese people have?

3. Would you like to travel on a high-speed train? What might you see out of the window in China?

INDEX

animals 8, 14, 16
Asia 4
capital 4
deserts 6
factories 16
farms 16
food 12, 14

forests 8
Great Wall of China 20
jobs 10, 16
mountains 6, 8
rivers 6
transport 18